The Breath of Merciful Spirit

Poems and Verses

★

Traumear

Paperback ISBN 978-1-7948-9501-0

*

www.traumear.com

The Breath of Merciful Spirit

1

Coming towards you at this crucial moment
You may look but not see, unless your seeing
Is caught up in much that deserves to be seen.

You may canter on four-legged beast to your goal
Or stand to attention for the exasperating news
From the well-oiled apparatus you call your art.

Those highly organized servants scrap their soul
Merely in order to experience that ice-wind,
Those flames that sear the kind heart mercilessly.

Then, also, one may gladly encourage them,
Speak to them gently, cajole their better selves
Out into the open, into day-knowing soul-domain.

If we knew how far good spirit sometimes reaches
Would we shy away from making our word count,
Respectful circus-performances notwithstanding?

Such an immense pressure builds up at times
And the harvest waits for no man to attend
But forces itself upon disreputable modernity.

Gladly the nerve-racking mountains are levelled,
The trickiest imponderables are untied by angels
While we make our intention to do good known.

*

2

Only since I am weak, unable to breathe easily,
Terrified of my own shadow, or so it seems,
Ready to wrangle with the elements, down under
The earth's magical confluences, does the mild,
Mannered spirit consider me worthy of influence.

Here peace settles disputes, takes issue with
Unborn sentiments, cancels the useless friendship,
While those who harbour grudges near the fringes
Take themselves off to the Spice Islands, there to
Bathe in memory's sun upon historic beaches.

We felt the time had come to empty our hearts
Of all rancour and this seemed to force the issue
For some in their humanist dream-world where
Nature's bodies had calcified, where trust made
Inroads on hearts but the ego cursed and stymied.

Swans crashed through the air then settled upon
Benign waters. This finally amounted to a fact,
Incontrovertibly linked to a million years of
Threadbare myth, however the golden bell had
Rung in the time of evolution and resurrection.

Some stood attentive, in small groups, beneath
Burgeoning crowns of oaks, their faces uplifted,
Gravity welcome as powerful urge to construction,
While others jogged after breakfast to settle their
Digestion and to blind life's organic demands.

*

3

Free yourself from all that brings darkness
By agreeing to all that brings light.
You may wish you were born before your time
And you wonder how you might influence fate,
However while you, in these waters, fish
You will discover better ways to wish.

There are so many ways to trust,
So many ways to be fair and just
And none oblige us to bestir ourselves
On behalf of gross emotion and cold calculation.
Energy never runs out, this must be learned by heart
And here we inculcate that thought in our art.

* * *

Speech practices

From the book 'Philology'

1

Verse

Verse rings true
and the table in front of me
floats on air as it were
because I too have succeeded
finally in safeguarding myself.

These few wicked moments,
sifted carefully out of life,
look for roots now.
I open the gates of my heart
And flowers are strewn.

But hatred wants its due.
We must rise out of ourselves.
Let us lift one another
not beyond spheres of temptation
nor out of harm's way,

ah, but into each other's bosom,
there to connect again,
sweetly to embrace.
Night uses me
horribly to descend in.

So gratitude urges itself
upon the still, white figure
trapped in late snow,
notwithstanding an eagerness
to be even more silenced.

*

2

the novel

One cannot come into one's own
by insisting on remaining alone,
one among many, ready to betray
what sunbeams mean and earthrays say –
one cannot do much in this way.

So shall we throw ourselves into the fray
and throw all caution to the wind?
Notion of higher and better thing?
Have so many past centuries lied
and now emergencies must invent

a brand new cause for every penny spent?
Rather let love gain an insight:
love nevertheless and love in spite
of untransformed or lurid light.
Let the new order march right in,

where heart shall be there head has been,
and many wives and husbands speak
of peace where formerly hell's hound
did throw into confusion and confound
the best we had which was not good.

Oh my, oh how our brain demands
a subtle recognition pure,
a cross to bear that saves, not thwarts,
nor would it roam in empty skies
but die as seed, not otherwise.

*

3

verse

The music weaving
spinthread cocoon
for mind's clear eye
carries its purpose
into man's crown.

We have sanctioned
too many simple causes
such as music mindful,
matter of music
such as my heart.

Under my power
all constraints fly,
all subtleties begin.
We shall not abhor
the miracle of selection.

By a god's leave
kisses are transformed,
gardens tended,
and foolishness rejects
overtures of foolishness.

I am acclaimed
by cloud through sunlight.
My acre fences in
most natural appetites
and reaps profusion.

*

4

the lyric

I am not ordinarily infatuated with created things
nor cold to the touch of desirable spirits.
My location in space is mundane.

Therefore prepare for my visit to your heart.
Extinguish no flame that would warm men
or erase lines of character from your face.

A glance through distance creates mountain ranges,
a more lingering look – satisfactory foothills,
red poplars cast out by an autumnal memory.

Help me sing these great colourful traditions,
for my voice trembles, searching the classified files,
my flesh tingles and would espouse ashes.

Take heart, child among children, or be weak
with a flair that announces joy to a wider world.
We have brought ourselves to these ends on purpose.

*

We cannot be outdone by a false moment
and superstitions with trite faces are overcome
by our unwillingness to carp at mere existence.

Out of the birch's skin springs the maiden,
from her mouth issue bitter prophesies
but her breasts promise the goodly pleasure.

I sink into myself as into earth,
willing to risk a learnéd life for a timc.
Wear this mask if you wish to accompany me.

Those caves once housed an absent mind,
smoke spiralled from burnt bone-fires
long beyond decades dedicated to cities.

Planes roar in skies emptied for the roar.
Flames leap up with sophisticated definition.
One lark nests angrily in the dried grass.

*

If this age were to reveal in black stone
its arrogance, in limned detail its mercenary
acts, should there be room to stand?

But a single affectation slyly expressed
suffices to cleanse the intentional market place,
to celebrate a thousand pieces of gold.

No one's business creates unnecessary contacts
while the horned beast rages over our roofs
and a spy stalks within, renting new territory.

And if we surely tempt a friend's presence,
we live to enjoy : we enjoy to live,
more than formerly aware of our gifts –

and handing wisdom on, not as wrapping
but as habits of homeliness, never statelier
than here in daylight, now in sight of one another.

* * *

1

Such misery as this
Is not good. I fail to see
What the purpose of such misery
Might be. I am even
Afraid to look and this may be
The main cause of this misery.

Oh very well, I shall peer
Into my conscience, into the
Inner workings of my soul,
In case something lurks there
That might explain
This 'hard rain'.

Here I have nothing to declare
And what I look at there
Flees from my gaze
As though it knew me
For a lost cause.
I may just give up hope.

I can imagine a beautiful garden,
I see tulips, fragrant daffodils
And in the corner a small
Barely trickling waterfall
Draws my gaze and I
Wonder why.

There are limits to how much
Misery we can take of such
All-embracing pain.
Here I go again,
Complaining when I should
Suffer and be still.

At times I get so angry
I could kill our cat when it
Gets in my way. This is sad.
The poor beasty never hurt
A fly. Although once
It brought me a dead robin.

I laid it on the window sill,
It looked so sweet,
Completely dead and at peace,
Its beak slightly open
As if it wanted to say:
I am content.

And that is the temperament
I generally despise.
When we're dead
That's no place to remain.
We should knock on that lid
And shout: Let me out!

So that is what I do now
But not a soul pays attention.
There seems to be, so
Far as I can see, a deplorable
Scarcity of souls
In this neck of the woods.

Nonetheless I keep knocking
Until my knuckles bleed.
Blood is a sign of life.
That occurred to me just now.
Where there's blood
There's life. Keep knocking.

* * *

2

Danny

Think of him as the captain
Of a liner and when he explains
The vast currents of sea and air,
His arms illustrate their destructive
Boon. Be sure he has been there
When death and life met on equal
Terms and surely he took notes
And secreted them in his cabin
Behind volumes of Hamsun and
Owen and Lawrence. Someone
Who injects into the modern world
Knowledge not encyclopaedic but
Personal and practical in the light
Of day – not mere daylight, sound
Bites and experimental test results –
Such a one is worth listening to.

However, the world's modern weight
Squats on our still enfeebled senses
So that all our loveliness might be
Wasted until we share it out
And expect no return. Danny
Has that down pat. He returns from
Voyages astral and maritime,
From inward explorations in caves
Where the soul prepares itself for
Those educational voyages and
Suddenly someone stands there
And has not yet tasted the freedom
Only human beings are worthy
To embrace and embody and now
The example is set of where we all
Would wish to be, on the open sea,
In no need of sea-change or landfall.

*

3

So you want to make a nuisance of yourself?
Why not limit you activities to the left
Or to the right, it's all the same, because
What you hate is that eternal centre ground.

*

Never thank your servant.
He is bound to get ideas above himself.

* *

4

Do please leave me in peace.
I don't want to hear any more.
If you have any complaints
from now on take them to headquarters.

There are arguments, there are disputes
which take on a life of their own.
Afterwards one wonders how it happened
that so much damage was done for nothing.

Male and female are ready to kill each other
at the slightest notice, for no reason.
One wonders how long it has to go on
before the penny drops: Modern is bad.

All the glorification of modernity
draws the last substance out of mankind.
Human beings are bound to stand alone
before their human god, stripped of pretence.

If I know what comes towards me
I can duck or open my arms.
All the subtleties of tradition and culture
are not worth one iota to the son of man.

We can prove we are innocent, we can
clear our name until no name is left.
Then we will be safe – without value,
untouchable, at liberty to 'freak out'.

*

5

What we think and do daily counts,
Like picking a strawberry for someone
Or eating it ourselves with awareness.

Then a lorry squashes our puppy or
Our wife comes down with cancer and
Its as if we had to start from scratch.

Directly above the earth a hundred stars
Could not care less about how we feel
So we look to each other, earth-blessed.

I don't know about you but my wish
Is for that sense of home here and now
With time for merriment and friendship.

*

6

When a husband mocks you,
When a wife insults you,
Then you know where you stand.
Or, on the other hand, you fall
Down among the other rubbish.
Wondering what has hit you.

Of course there are umpteen
Modern schemes and devices
For circumnavigating this issue.
Don't love or care to begin with,
Just concentrate on what you like
And hide away in your hell.

Then the colloquial world moves
To China where hell is fumigated
And a million sticky buns lie
Untasted by the side of the road,
Food for the rat and the toad –
As if that were cause for concern.

Evil is a dose of heart-burn
And betimes we need the reminder
There's still work to be done.
We have to keep the blues on the run.
The sheer tenacity of genius
Is game for the devil anytime.

*

7

When Moses on the mountain stood
of course he wanted to be good
and said: „Wie nah fühl ich mich dir,“
so full was he of ego-brew,
but then was overcome by fear
when told: „Du gleichst dem Geist den du
begreifst, nicht mir.“
The universal lord observed
how suddenly his courage swerved
and sent him one to make amends,
saying: “This one has laws galore
and in his name my spirit sends
what all you need to live, and more,
until your stiff neck bends.”

*

8

You are welcome, I said,
you have slept all night
and oh what a struggle!
Now tighten you belt.

He reached out with his hand,
Firmly he encircled my waist.
This was no stranger to sin,
Merely a refuse collector.

Oh he was a giant of a man,
Ever pursued by the elements,
His brain a mass of wires
And flames poured from his eyes.

I admired his long grey beard
And suppressed all my emotion.
This, it seemed, was my father,
Gathering the universe to himself.

Clinging to his gown, the tiny
People were eating thorns,
Like goats on Cretan hillsides
In view of the Libyan sea.

*

9

There has been so much silly talk
about the seventh seal, and now they
activate the machine in their brain
in order to make themselves happy.

*

I stood high above the city, the scent of
roses in my nostrils and my fingers clasping
those of the one who had sought me out
in spite of the foul lies spread about me.

*

Look, you must try to understand with your
entire body that she who leapt to your defence
had conquered her fear and as a consequence,
in the clouds – all those images of wild horses.

*

Under a microscope I suddenly came upon
the message that we must try to escape
rather than amuse ourselves with cheap
references to a time when we still lived.

*

No road now where once I had danced through
groves of birches and no longer does the air
smell of the rich soil but the seagulls still roam
through untroubled space above our heads.

*

He said he had run you of patience and since he
believed in neither god nor himself how could he
resist the temptation to end his life by hiding
in a ditch where he hoped never to be found.

*

The gold in our soul has been melted by grief
and we spring into action for no good reason
while the earth trembles beneath our feet,
deeply disturbed by the popular remonstrances.

*

It had happened so long ago that we had hoped
the world might have forgotten, especially since
no one had discovered whose blood was spilled,
whose mouth was stopped, whose heart broken.

*

You turn left at the church unless
the door is open and the singing
tickles your fancy, then you may
recall the burden of your childhood.

*

We were skating to music, round and round,
when suddenly I reached across for her hand
and we cheerfully skated in perfect ignorance
of who we were and of why we must part.

*

Close eyes, let force of nature
Grip the vitals. Then relax a moment.
You have organized nothing.
Therefore spin your thread.

*

Sometimes I need to draw blood.
At last that is how it seems.
I shall not take it seriously.
Morning after morning I die.

* * *

10

Six sonnets

1

The moment is not ripe for me to wonder
Exactly how to love and how to know.
Day in day out I stay within and ponder
The secret of my life – and how I grow.

Much liveliness of spirit is required
In order to become what one would be.
You may be dull or you may feel inspired –
It all comes down to your humanity.

Therefore the odd illusion is no thing
To be rejected for the sake of truth.
You know that each experience would bring
You closer to your love, as in your youth

You dallied with conceptions of the last
Retreat until the final die was cast.

*

2

Oh save us from the weakness of the flesh
When it denies us as we would expect
And then insists on its own course of action.

The misery of pain, and its protraction
Must find us all too eager to protect
Our status – when experience would refresh.

There's one transition that inspires fear
When on our own behalf we start to bleed,
While images of life would fade from view.

The time has come to think and to renew
What makes us grow, and what we really need
To be and to become, both now and here.

Let heart and head be one and make no fuss
And bless the difference between them and us.

*

3

So much that I have dreamt in years gone by
Was prophecy, to tap the future source.
It seems we underestimate the force
Of youthful thought while every girl or guy

Stays put in primal consciousness all day
And has no inkling of the wrath to come.
Feeling, reflection – all by rule of thumb –
Take precedence, and chase all grief away.

Then from on high an energy presumes
To lock the tardy traveller in a cell
And throws the key away – we know it well –
While here, within the blind heart, panic looms.

What luck that years ago one man extracted
The sting from death because of how he acted.

*

4

Have I come through? Have my fears
Borne fruit? Has the one I prayed
For assistance opened doors?
Oh that by fault I have ploughed

Many a furrow in vain
Or at least so it seems when at last
The piper has piped his tune
And those who were least received most.

Lost, the faithless heart,
Blinded the careless eye
And the one who would hold court
Knows he gains nothing now.

Ah but we who have loved
Understand now why we grieved.

*

5

The living light descends upon my brain
That I may see that which has not been seen
And speak of it, and never speak in vain.

I have been told my voice's edge is keen
But this is as it seems, and yet true
For my great weakness must be overcome.

The gulf that opens between me and you
Gives berth to those who live by rule of thumb
And where they tread in time will roses bloom.

And nothing more than this is ever needed,
For where they live is ample living-room
And space that went for centuries unheeded.

We strike the balance and we hold the feast,
for those who loved me most have suffered least.

*

6

Do but prepare for the great reception
For him whose love is as rain upon soil.
What you may think of as grim interruption
Must introduce you to love without fail.

Lately the sunlight, that shuns all fault,
Gives to the earth a brand new splendour.
Only those who have justly dealt
With worldly law can bear the thunder.

Etched into bark and carved into stone,
Signs of the times the time reveal.
Ah but the final word – benign –
Limits the record, pole to pole

And the pendulum swings in praise of earth
That all who have value may know their worth.

* * * (02/06/20)

11

Three Sonnets

1

Though she left my heart in tatters,
As the saying goes, I know,
Love's the only thing that matters
As we find ourselves and grow.

Oh she knew what she was doing,
So my vanity insists
And the tenure of her wooing
Is the devil she enlists.

This is nothing, and I smile,
Trapped in my superior way.
This is falsehood, I revile
Everything she has to say.

Both of us are being tested –
Neither one is good or bested.

*

2

I bend and will not break,
Have learned this to my shame.
Like all who would awake
I praise his glorious name.

I hurt and do not cry
For I would silent be.
All secrets by and by
Are published and set free.

Oh massively there's cause
For holding forth out loud.
In spite of written laws
There's chaos for the crowd.

We gain a special hearing
Even for just appearing.

*

3

I praise the Jesus who upheld the law
Of eternal life right to the bitter end,
so we may see now too the things he saw
Or good pretend and better love forefend.

How strange, that one in whom our memory rests
Should seem so close to us in sleep and waking!
How precious what our intellect invests
In his so overstated undertaking!

I'll not be swayed by those who draw his life
Into contempt, his name through streets dogmatic,
While in their hearts survival's law is rife
And what they say remains inert and static.

What he accomplished, let it be our choice
And argue who he was with lesser voice.

* * *

12

Four Sonnets

1

A little insight into personality
arranges a few facts.
We are too nervous for the totality
which directs and attracts.

A lyrical moment however,
when we feel we might dissociate
ourselves from strange pain, can never
abstract love from hate.

The noise must abate in any case.
Once we have tasted
time we must also try space.
So much talent is wasted.

For myself I value clean air
And a fresh wind blowing my hair.

*

2

She stepped on the bridge as though
eventually she intended to cross.
We were all waiting below
hopeful, though mostly at a loss.

Halfway across will she hesitate
and express the pleasure of anxiety
or shall we say it's too late?
Nothing like a bit of variety.

Now as she turns and smiles,
small wonder we breathe a sigh
of relief, for her smile beguiles.
She is ill informed. So am I.

Give it a few days and then
you may taste the power of the pen.

*

3

The night leans in across the sash,
the scent of horses and of rain,
the distant shrieking of a train,
the memory of a car crash –

Look to yourself now. Those
who dream of a career may still
come to their senses. We overfill
the brain with facts as it grows.

Also in the woods a late deer
bellows its request for a mate
and the pines insist its too late
to conquer hope and fear.

A blackbird singing in its sleep.
Leviathan rising from the deep.

*

4

He loved, but with an eye to her consent
which meant that in her heart she had no hold,
no tenure, when her temperament was spent,
so in return she turned into a scold.

Therefore it would appear he was at fault,
for love would enter in the loved one's soul
unquestioningly, not waiting to be called;
when crossing bridges having to pay toll.

However it would seem that in her haste
to judge to be not judged she overstepped
heart's ease, so her affection was not chaste
but either pushy or in handcuffs kept.

Let him but take his courage in his hand
and her to learn that love would be unplanned.

* * * *

13

She tears herself away from all the chores
and comes across all love and tender care
and shrouded in a mist – which he deplores.
This is the time for him to be aware.

The squirrels on the lawn refuse to budge.
A magpie knows it's time to fly away.
The rain has stopped. He eats a piece of fudge
because it rhymes – as it did yesterday.

She searches for her love among the clouds
where someone comes who promised to arrive.
Then she complains there are too many crowds
for girls in love and pleasure to survive.

He limits his concern to half an hour.
She takes a nap – and afterwards a shower

*

14

And then I took me down to where my friends
Had all escaped the onslaught of the waves
And there they sat, around the campfire, dreaming
Of times when we would all be in our graves –
But that is not how this or that world ends.

We waited for the night to have its say,
For clouds to hide the moon and all the stars,
And then we knew the tiger would appear,
Its gliding show of black and yellow bars,
And it would frighten all our fears away.

So that was how it happened. First it slew
The goat, for we had tied it to a pole
As bait. And then we shot it through the head
And threw the corpse into that anxious hole
That often gapes between my love and you.

Now I was on my own again. It seemed
That where the jungle and the beach within
My breast were one – a single symbol which
Could be relied on – I might soon begin
Beauty's delight, of which I daily dreamed.

Alas, the Christ I knew had other plans
And let me know in no uncertain terms
That there was still a great deal to be suffered:
No illness due to viruses or germs
But nature elemental, mortal man's.

*

15

Deny yourself, they say, and they deny
The very one who said that they should love
His little ones, and therefore, by and by,
The wrath they flee attacks them from above.

They mortify the flesh and they suppose
This brings them closer to the god who poured
His spirit on all flesh. God only knows
How much the son of man their deeds abhorred.

These monks and nuns, who sold their souls to wrath
And children from misguided girls who erred,
Shall suffer without doubt the aftermath
Until their greater error is transferred

By those who have believed in god from birth –
And then remove all falsehood from the earth

*

16

The racist slur is flung from mouth to ear,
And by the thoughtless ones from heart to soul,
And they presume they play a righteous role,
When they but spread anxiety and fear.

One thing alone is needful, that we learn
To value difference, whether bad or good.
Difference informs us but we know we would
Be harmed in time by selfish likelihood.

The man I hate but shows me my own fault,
Which I would mend, if I but cared for him.
By choosing kind I go out on a limb
Which breaks when my judgmental name is called.

Oh the reward is theirs who choose to labour
Within their souls to love their racist neighbour.

*

17

Hate begets hate, love love, that's all I know.
Those who would mend the world and in their hearts
Remain unholy, exchange blow for blow
And multiply their own disjointed parts.

If we but knew it, we are merely tools
While we impress upon the world our fears
Which accident in no time overrules.
Our image is not quite as it appears.

Know those who voice the opposite concern,
Who flip the coin again until it shows
Heads for our tails, and righteously they burn
Our righteous flags, as every martyr knows.

Oh no, it makes no sense, this blind pursuit
Of empty virtues by some unknown route.

*

18

He wondered who he was right to the end
And this was not exactly what he'd planned.
At times it seemed his mind refused to bend
Before the storm. He kept the upper hand

Where children shouted and demanded love
From those endowed with neither heart nor brain.
Their slippery verbiage entered from above
Where institution reigned. They used the cane

To get their own back when they felt absurd,
For there was very little they could offer.
The real questions asked were never heard
And what was heard was hidden in the coffer

Of memory that would long outlast these days
Of wounded pride and effort that betrays.

*

19

Of course I know exactly who I am.
The little bit of ignorance inside me
Has never had the right amount of room
Or common education to provide me

With justified excuses, that I might
Demand an explanation from the State
For how they treat me sometimes when I'm late
Or when it's cold and I forgot my coat.

Good gracious! Man alive! Who would have thought
That underneath that little bit of varnish
Her mood would hold! So I, with all my might,
So that my sudden outburst would not tarnish

Her soul, insisted that she learn my name
And memorize for all time whence I came.

*

20

It could be that I hold myself too dear
For many of the tasks that come my way.
Too often I am stuck for what to say
Because I hope – I fail – and then I fear.

At certain times I let my will be known
As if there were some virtue in the act,
The mere concession to an ill-based fact,
And then I wonder, is that face my own?

There must be some conceit in every thought
Not based on faith nor in affection bound.
While my imagination is unsound,
I cannot make my words mean what they ought

The rarest thing on earth is truthful being
Anchored in each days feeling, hearing, seeing.

*

21

As though you knew which way to turn
When confronted by the Chinese dragons,
You deliver yourself up to the spirits
Of the power and might within,
Not caring what mood they're in,
As long as they plague you for good reason
And not to aggrandize themselves, because
In that case you'd better leave them sitting
On the shelf beside that blue vase which
Looks good next to anything at all.

If you accuse me of avoiding the point
I have to tell you that you're wrong.
For how long have I not told poets not to
Meddle with the language of the herd.
You yourself drink from the fountain,
And is it ever too crowded there?
I think you'll agree that the further you look
Off into the distance the more does the
Smoke blow into your face. Why not
Exasperate scientists and church-goers?

*

22

I am perfectly content in my community
And hope the same for you. I have the feeling
That your claws are out, your teeth on edge.
Am I wrong about that? I hope so.
The logic of our existence nowadays
Reminds me of a fox outside a chicken coop
Waiting for the owner to open up, but this is
Surely a bit silly. The owner's shotgun
Hangs by a nail just inside the barn door.

Shall I be going on a holiday this year?
I always wonder what such a question has to
Do with reality. Are we not all in the same mess?
No, that is surely an exaggeration. Now the fox
Trots off. I can relax. I dislike bloodshed.
I stand here in a field of wheat. Thunder clouds
Gathering over the mountains and larks
No longer ascend, jubilating, while my heart
Clings to a revolting memory.

*

23

New Poems

1

Because my hand shakes
should that get me down?
Because of these searing cramps
I would rather not sleep
but remain watchful.
One never knows, a time of ease
Might be just around the corner.

*

2

Please do not leave me,
companion of my life.
Left on my own, would I not
transfer my affection
to matters of no account?

Oh, what I have to give
is not now wanted
and what is wanted I
cannot give. Nonetheless
I would work and live.

*

3

Where roses lead a life of their own
and apples hang heavy and full –
there you and I spent an hour
wisely in each others company.

It was well known by the neighbours
that our companionship was chaste,
nonetheless they chatted behind the fence,
for that is how neighbours behave.

I am done with understanding. I shall
praise the few years I have left
and try to get in no one's way,
while storms ravage the earth.

*

4

These horrors frighten me.
I am bereft of common sense.
All was foretold, nonetheless
one captures the moment's stillness
in the hope of energetic innocence.

If you come here on a windy day
let not your spirits flag
for care is taken to capture
the noisome disturber of our peace.
During that great chorus of light –
new I grafted upon the old.

*

5

If it were up to me I would
catch my enemy by the throat
and despatch him. However
no ammount of ferocity serves.

The very clanging of kitchen utensils
signals what we have awaited
and the door slamming shuts out
the voice that persuades to prayer.

*

6

If you wish to impress me
why not devote your time on earth
to the ‘playful garb’. This is
clothing only those can see
who transform each moment into
time’s contemporary perspective.

However it may happen that,
livid and frantic one day,
you will seek to populate the moon
and nonetheless you will find
that I have prepared land for you
and await your transient population.

*

7

As soon as anxiety surfaces,
the best thing to do is relax.
Think of a beautiful woman,
of a man you can trust who acts.

Trade in your harmless possessions
for rifles and hand grenades
and declare your own moratorium
on the manners of lads and maids.

Over against life's eternal
repetition of goods for use,
suddenly what you are offered
is a deal you cannot refuse.

Alas, the illusion of fervour
masks the contention at heart,
when out of the blue a new moon
persuades you to stop and restart.

These are all handy tips
for gradually drawing to a close
and handing over to the landlord
all those anxieties you chose.

*

8

It may well be the case that if I have
Nothing of importance to say at present
Something wishes to say me,
So I position myself fortuitously.
After all, groundwater rises
Or sinks depending on atmosphere
And an electric current searches
For the quickest route back to earth.
So I take a deep breath and climb.

* * *

24

Through all my fashions and disguises
I seek to follow you. And should I win
prizes for delicious fruit ripened,
these I accept before I continue in

my leisurely pursuit of you here
and now. I too have humanity
and would appear, for that reason,
to be no enemy of urbanity.

All that I value at heart's ease
reflects your image and your wise
release of all that would interfere
with your beauty, joy and good cheer.

You are the dancer whose steps I
memorize, then fashion and disguise.

*

25

1

I'm no longer sure, should I
Complain about getting stuck
In this maze, in these dire
Consequences of having consented
To the burial of the Prince of love?
While he was still above ground
I believe I did my level best
To believe in victory and conquest
At any cost, even when the light
Went out for weeks at a time.
Oh yes, there were moments
When I dreaded the very thought
Of continuing to exist among
The local natives. Their bellicose
Spirit, the fact that they had
Massacred, in their madness,
Their children and then composed
Ditties in praise of their
Secular institutions, accounted
For the hell they were in.
I threw all records in the bin
And went for a long drive.
There's this I can say about being
Alive in this decisive century –
It's an adventure. It appeals
To my nature as I know it.
Welcome Hades then, if it
Means what I think it means,
Namely escape from this stink.
Writing about it is a waste of ink.
Love is dead and gone and I
Bring the shades down on this
Vicarious excuse of a world.

*

2

When love is but a word and nought
Counts for nought, I fold my tent
And give it not another thought
That all my waking hours were spent

In hot pursuit of fickle truth,
Belligerent when the time was ripe,
Society's clown and most uncouth
When conversation ran to type.

Of course it always seemed unjust
That only fools were allowed to flee
When truth was trampled in the dust
As cover-up for bastardy.

It seems that what the world now needs
Is trumpery, sham and lies for deeds.

*

3

Darkness descends on the world.
In a moment, all that made life
Seem worthwhile buckles,
Slides into oblivion. I make
My peace with the confusion.

You too seem intent on sweeping
Lust and the sentiments under the table.
Trade-winds on the open ocean
Fan no merchants into port but
Dictate a riot of self-sufficiency.

*

4

You help me with each step I take
And every moment I survive
I tranquillize the ritual moods
And spit on the subservient drive.

But when the virulent trumpet sounds
I'm on my own and know it well
And lift my courage to the stars –
Suspending judgment for a spell –

Until you let me know that love
Has once more risen from the soil
To quench the thirst, to satisfy
The soul that without love must spoil.

* * *
* *
*

Index of first lines in alphabetic order

* * *

www.ingramcontent.com/pod-product-compliance
Ingram Content Group UK Ltd.
Pitfield, Milton Keynes, MK11 3LW, UK
UKHW042010190726
13854UKWH00005B/2233